A

LETTER

ADDRESSED TO THE

HON. JOHN LYNCH,

CHAIRMAN OF THE

SPECIAL CONGRESSIONAL COMMITTEE

OF THE UNITED STATES SENATE,

ON THE

NAVIGATION INTEREST:

ADVOCATING THE EXPEDIENCY OF PURCHASING

IRON SHIPS AND STEAMERS

IN SCOTLAND,

BEING THE RESULT OF A RECENT VISIT AND EXTENDED OBSERVATION

BY

CAPT. JOHN CODMAN.

BOSTON:
A. WILLIAMS & COMPANY,
135 WASHINGTON STREET,
1869.

A LETTER

ADDRESSED TO THE

HON. JOHN LYNCH,

CHAIRMAN OF THE

SPECIAL CONGRESSIONAL COMMITTEE

OF THE UNITED STATES SENATE,

ON THE

NAVIGATION INTEREST:

ADVOCATING THE EXPEDIENCY OF PURCHASING

IRON SHIPS AND STEAMERS

IN SCOTLAND,

BEING THE RESULT OF A RECENT VISIT AND EXTENDED OBSERVATION

BY

CAPT. JOHN CODMAN.

BOSTON:
A. WILLIAMS & COMPANY,
135 WASHINGTON STREET,
1869.

THESE investigations in Scotland were made at the request of the New York Board of Underwriters, and the result is thus presented with the hope that it may attract not only the attention of the Congressional Committee, but also that of the general public.

BARKER, COTTER & CO., PRINTERS, 14 STATE STREET.

DUMBARTON ON THE CLYDE,
November 15, 1869.

SIR:—I propose, with your kind permission, to ask your attention to some remarks and statistics touching the rise and fall of the American merchant marine, and to some suggestions, or rather a single suggestion—for the renewal of its prosperity. Little can be added in the way of argument, to what I have often written for commercial newspapers in Boston and New York, upon this subject, but new facts are every day corroborating the views advanced years ago, and these still point to the same—the only remedy.

More than twenty years since, the relative advantages of wood and iron in the construction of ships, and especially of steamers, were discussed by some anonymous writer and myself in the columns of the *New York Journal of Commerce.* My opponent favored the former material, and when, as I flattered myself, he was driven to the wall in the discussion of durability, cargo space, and danger from lightning, he fell back upon what he considered incontrovertible at any rate, "Wood is buoyant, iron is not, when waterlogged;" forgetting that a steamer of any kind must have machinery in her, the weight of which with the addition of the rest of her capacity being occupied by water, would surely sink her. There was one argument however then used against iron, which I was bound to admit had a certain force, but which has lost much of its force since that time,—I mean the quick fouling of iron bottoms. In those days, dockage was rare and expensive, and was scarcely to be obtained at all, especially for large ships, excepting in a very few of the ports of Europe and America. At this time, although it must be confessed that no lasting coating for iron has been discovered, still the facilities for docking all over the world have so increased that this difficulty is infinitely less; and science has also disposed effectually of the vagaries of the compass.

Time has therefore settled one great point for us. Iron is better than wood, and the proof of it is, that all nations excepting the United States use the iron in preference. Our people do not use it, because iron and the labor on iron are too costly, and because not being able consequently to build iron vessels ourselves, our ridiculously absurd navigation laws prevent us from purchasing such ships, and we thus deliberately throw the trade in them into the hands of the nation that can build them cheapest, and into those of others like the Germans, who buy their ships in England. Our action *quo ad hoc* is neither more nor less than national suicide!

I am appealing through you to our government for a repeal of the present odious law—a law which expressly forbids us to hoist the American flag on any vessel that is not built on American soil, and launched into American waters. It is not a party question. I almost wish that it was, for then it would commend itself to the ambition of some politician. It concerns equally the democrat and the republican, and paradoxical as it may seem, the free trade men and the protectionists alike. For the present law, while clearly in opposition to free trade, *protects foreigners instead of our own people.* Yes we *protect* the British, German, and French shipowners, captains, engineers, crews and their families, insurance companies, ship-chandlers, and even the shipbuilders and machinists who do their repairs at home instead of in our yards—*against ourselves!*

When last in New York one of our first shipbuilders told me that he wished the law repealed, because, he said, "our business is now so nearly dead, that it is worth nothing, whereas if our merchants owned the ships that came into this port, we should have ten times more work to do in repairing than we now have in building." I know that there are certain antiquated shipbuilders on the eastern shore, of whom the newspapers report occasionally that they have built a fine schooner or possibly a bark or a ship, (for the coasting trade in almost every instance,) who innocently suppose that the abrogation of the law would be an injury to them, and their little parish; and who moreover flatter themselves that if they can get Congress to lessen the duty on copper and hemp they can compete with iron hulls and wire rigging! Accordingly they make periodical journeys to Washington, perhaps to find General Jackson. But Congress pays no attention to these old fogies. To afford them relief, it would be obliged to do much more than they ask. The duties should not only be taken off from copper and hemp, but iron and coal mines should be established in their neighborhood for their express convenience, their workmen should be obliged to labor for one dollar per day — all internal and inward revenue dues should be abolished for all articles consumed by their families, and their people should give up their roast beef, and live on porridge! When all this comes to pass the Maine shipbuilder can perhaps after a few years experience compete with the Scotsman.

Possibly they would be the gainers in the long run, if like Mr. Briggs, whom we all remember as one of our best Boston shipbuilders, they should take a run over here, and after looking at the work going on, come home again, and selling out their stock in trade, go into some other business. At most the Maine shipbuilders build only for the coasting trade, and if it were deemed advisable that the whole country should suffer for their supposed benefit, the law might be abrogated in so far only as relates to foriegn trade, leaving the coasting trade to be still carried on in American built vessels. Protectionists would then have nearly all they have now, for it is notorious, and the marine columns of the newspapers bear daily witness to the fact that nearly all our foreign trade is carried on in foreign bottoms. This we cannot help, for so long as the treaties with England, France, Germany and other countries exist, our merchants cannot be prevented from importing their merchandise in the cheapest manner. We may still keep up our coasting monopoly, and thus oblige merchants and ultimately consumers to pay more for their goods than if cheaper vessels were allowed to carry them. We may for the sake of benefiting Pennsylvania iron, force our railroads to use it, even if English iron could be imported for half the money. But this class of protectionists although exercising an unlimited amount of tyranny on our own highways, seem to forget that they cannot control the ocean, which is the highway of the world! In order to do that, they must abolish all treaties, and enact a law that none other than vessels under the American flag shall enter our ports. The result of such "protection" as this would be, that American vessels would not be allowed to enter foreign ports, and all the European trade would be carried on through Canada and thence in British bottoms.

But we must take facts as we find them. Our produce is carried in British built ships from our ports. Our merchants ship and receive almost all their goods in British built ships, and what is most humiliating of all, our government pays subsidies to daily lines of British built steamers under foreign flags, and no subsidy to any transatlantic line of our own, and our people when they go abroad or return home, can never see the stars and stripes waving over their heads — because, and all because we insist on *protecting* — whom? why the foreigners instead of ourselves!

In the old days of wooden sailing ships, of cheap living, and of comparatively cheap labor in the United States, our mechanics advanced so rapidly in skill of workmanship and in perfection of model, that the English shipbuilders were not only rivalled, but far outstripped in the race. Though her navy was still the largest in the world, the commercial marine of England was vastly inferior in speed, symmetry and discipline, to the American, and was fast yielding to it in amount of tonnage.

Who does not remember our magnificent liners and China clippers? Our ships were built cheaper and better than they could be built in England, and therefore English merchants preferred to ship their cargoes in them rather than in British bottoms, because they could afford to carry the goods at a cheaper rate. They acted precisely as our merchants act now. But did their government act like ours? On the contrary, it saw its commerce declining, its seamen becoming Americans, and thus depriving their native land of their services in case of war, while American shipowners were making the profit on freights that Englishmen before had made.

At that time the navigation laws of England were the same as ours now are, and moreover, she had a powerful and influential body of shipbuilders to contend against, which we have not. Still, in face of the difficulty, and even with the necessity of bringing temporary disaster on a class for the good of the nation, the English wisely abolished their system of protection, and gave their merchants the liberty to come to the United States for their supply of ships.

Neither was there any eventual loss to the builders, for they turned their attention to iron; and now the wooden clippers and packets are dying out, as no more of them are being built, and the age of wood and sails has given place to the age of iron and steam. These are revolutions in the nature of things that old fogyism cannot stop, any more than it can stop the revolution of the earth by holding a handspike against the sun!

If we examine the statistics of English and American vessels engaged in foreign trade, we shall find that in the year 1858 they were about equal, being in round numbers 5,500,000 tons each. After that time the British tonnage gradually increased, and the American tonnage slowly decreased in comparison, till the year 1860, when the war put the finishing stroke to our commercial marine, and in 1867–1868, the English tonnage had run up to nearly 8,000,000, and ours had fallen off to 4,300,000. This includes inland, river and lake navigation. So nearly as can be estimated, the tonnage engaged in foreign trade was less than 1,300,000, the exact statistics being at the close of the year 1868.—

Shipping on the Lakes.	695,694
" on the Rivers,	481,217
" on the Pacific,	166,512
" on the Atlantic and Gulf, (the greater part coastwise.)	2,974,975
	4,318,398

By some, this will be accounted for in two ways. First, by the transfer of many of our ships to the British flag, as a security against the rebel cruisers; and secondly, by the raids of the "Alabama" and her consorts. Doubtless both these causes have something to do with the matter; but the first is not of its supposed importance, and the latter is almost infinitesimal. For a better judgment of fact, let any one who has eyes survey our deserted shipyards, and then come over here, and look at the business doing upon the Clyde alone.

It was an occasion and an era, when, two years ago, thousands of people went from Boston to Newburyport to see two steamers launched, which were to compete successfully with the Cunard and Inman ships for the carrying trade to Liverpool. They are still lying at the docks, overwhelmed with debt contracted in their short career. Here, you will see ships of equal size launched almost every week, and attracting so little attention that the neighboring workmen do not cease from their labor as these vessels slip from the ways! That their business is profitable is evident by their increase.

I have taken the statistics of 1867 from a document issued by our government. Since that time, while our shipyards have been as idle as before, those of Great Britain have been increasing their business in a greater ratio than ever. Taking, therefore, into consideration the losses by perils of the sea, which have not been replaced on our side, we can scarcely have at this day more tonnage engaged in foreign trade than at the close of 1868, while Great Britain cannot fall short of 9,000,000 tons, including the amount she has built and sold to Germany and other foreign countries.

If we continue in the same track of downward progression or standstill, it will not be many years before our commercial marine shall become nearly extinct. If we resolve that this shall be so, because our country having extended into the interior so vastly that our seaboard is not of the importance it once was, and, therefore, we have no further need of ships or of sailors, let us allow the humiliating fact at once, and call no more meetings for the consideration of the revival of our commerce.

I was about to say, let us become Chinese or Japanese, and admit to other civilized nations that they only are competent to perform the carrying trade for us. But I will not do the Chinese and Japanese such injustice. Even these nations, just emerging from barbarism, entertain no such suicidal doctrine of "protection" as we do. *Be it remembered that the United States is the only nation, civilized or uncivilized,* upon the face of the earth, that puts an absolute prohibition upon the purchase of a foreign ship by its people!

Are we, because circumstances beyond our control, — such as the substitution of iron for wood, and because the taxes that civil war has brought upon us have made us unable to compete with England in shipbuilding,—are we to refuse to buy her ships for our use, especially when there is no possible interest of our own that we can injure by so doing?

The question before us is, whether by our present policy of supine indifference we shall suffer our merchant marine to be totally annihilated. If we take that resolution we may as well abolish the navy likewise, for it will have no commerce to protect. And yet we must perforce support a larger navy than ever before in time of peace, because in time of war we shall want sailors. What manner of economy is this?

Before the late war we had one of the largest commercial marines in the world, and, considering the importance of that, one of the smallest navies. Now we have a powerful navy and very little commerce. I well remember when in command of a ship in the harbor of Rio de Janeiro twenty years ago, and loading coffee with forty other American vessels, how one old sailing frigate was considered protection enough for all of us on the whole coast of Brazil. Three years since I was again in that port in a steamer, and mine was the only American flag that flew there, excepting those of seven gunboats and frigates and of an iron-clad, whose only "protegé" was the little "Tijuca."

Yes, what manner of economy is this? If we will not have merchantmen we *must* have men-of-war. When the late war broke out, small as our navy was in its numbers of men and ships, it was instantly recruited to its full requirement of sailors from the merchant service, which also supplied steamers and sailing vessels for its first need. Remember, too, that until these men were wanted, they were adding to the industry of the country by earning wages, paid them by merchants *for value received*, whereas we are now obliged to pay them for *no* real value received. In other words, a great part of the money disbursed for navy appropriations might be saved, and an equal amount might be gained to the country in the produce of labor, so that we virtually not only spend unnecessarily these amounts, but the double of them. Surely from both points of view, the necessity of a supply of men, and the economy of maintaining this supply, the restoration of our commercial marine is worthy of consideration.

I am aware that it has been proposed to introduce a bill into Congress allowing our merchants to buy foreign vessels upon the payment of a duty. This scheme must have emanated from the brain of some one who cannot have given the subject due consideration. We claim, to use a treaty phrase, "to be put on the footing of the most favored nations." Duties are levied for revenue and for protection. This is not a case for either. If Congress will not abrogate the law *in toto*, there will be no revenue from such a source as proposed, for we cannot afford to buy the ships and to compete with other nations, unless we have the same facilities that they have. In this competition for the carrying trade, with the rest of the world, we must have nothing whatever to hold us back in the race, especially as the long continued indifference of our government has left us already far astern. We must have ships duty free, and also ship's stores out of bond, as in England.

As to protecting any home interests I think it has been already demonstrated that there are none to protect. But if our antidiluvian arkwrights still object, maintaining as they do at this late day, like my friend in the "Journal of Commerce" more than twenty years since, that wood is preferable to iron — then let an exception be made in their favor, let iron, steel and composite ships only, be admitted duty free to our flag, and let the law remain as it is, so far as wooden vessels are concerned. They will still have the market of the world before them, for not only will we buy their vessels of them, if we find them cheaper, and more profitable than iron, but the English, who have no prohibitory law, will do likewise. I have not heard however that any orders have gone out lately from this country to America for wooden ships. There is certainly nothing that looks like it upon the Clyde.

In the mean time, it may not be amiss for them to look over the estimates of Mr. Donald McKay, a well-known shipbuilder of Boston, and a born Scotsman I believe withal — at any rate, a man of thrift and business capacity. He estimates the customs duties upon the articles required for a wooden ship of 1,000 tons, at $8,665.33 in gold. Let them put that into their calculations, and then add one hundred per cent. for the difference in labor against them, and moreover find some means of stretching a wooden ship to the capacity of one of iron, and of making wood equally durable, before they solicit any order from this side.

There are certain things upon which we form such fixed opinions, that we wonder that argument is necessary to convince those whom we wish to influence. This subject is one of them, and yet it is not very surprising that while the arguments I have used are still uncontroverted, so little interest is felt in the matter. It appeals to the individual interest of no one. It is everybody's business, — therefore it is nobody's. What little individual interest there is, is exercised against it, by that very small class of short sighted shipbuilders that I have referred to, who imagine that they would suffer injury, by a repeal of the navigation laws, and whose few votes seem to be of sufficient consequence for the whole nation to suffer on their account. As I have already hinted, the importers and shippers are supremely indifferent about it. Patriotism with them, generally, is a motive secondary to individual profit and convenience. They can now ship and import all they desire, and they care not under what flag it is done.

I shall still further, with the aid of figures which are said never to lie, endeavor to place the subject before you in such a light, that the correctness of these views cannot but be acknowledged, although people may not choose to interest themselves in what does not personally concern them. I have been lately spending some months in Scotland and more particularly at Dumbarton on the Clyde, where I have had ample opportunities for observing the immense amount of work going on in shipbuilding upon that river, and of making the acquaintance of gentlemen engaged in it at Glasgow, Greenock and Dumbarton.

The object of this essay is to convince my countrymen by argument, — which, I hope, has already been done, — that our present navigation laws are onerous and useless, and then to show by authentic statistics that the Clyde is the natural ship-producing district of the world. It is as much so as the valley of the Mississippi is intended by nature for the supply of grain. That it is the region for such production is allowed by Great Britain. Therefore, she wisely admits all cereals duty free, because she cannot produce them herself in sufficient quantity for her own consumption. Let us imitate her policy in supplying ourselves with a necessity equally imperative.

I shall now proceed to show that the capacity of this locality to supply the world with ships at the cheapest rates, has not been overestimated. The advantages of the Clyde consist in its location, its well organized system of labor, the cheapness of iron and coal which are both abundant upon its banks, the economical habits of the workmen, whose requirements are so small that they are satisfied with moderate wages, and in the determination and the ability also to underbid the whole world in contracts for shipbuilding.

It is not many years since the Clyde was an insignificant stream, insignificant at least as regarded everything but its history, and the beauty of its surrounding scenery. In those days of wooden ship-building, Greenock at its mouth was a place of some commercial importance, while the shallow water opposite Dumbarton and Glasgow, excluded these towns from any participation in the prosperity of their more fortunate neighbor. But of late years the whole river has been dredged, so that at this day, vessels drawing twenty-one feet, can reach the wharves of Glasgow with ease.

If you would observe the work that is going on, you should take a steamer at the bridge in Glasgow, and after passing the quays crowded with shipping, you will see upon either bank for miles, steamers and sailing vessels in process of construction, and your ears will be almost deafened with the din of hammers and machinery. There are but intervals of quiet between Glasgow, Renfrew, Dumbarton, Port Glasgow and Greenock, all of which places are alive with this one industry.

Upon an average there are about twenty thousand workmen employed, and when the prolific nature of this population is considered, it may be computed that their families count eighty thousand more. Besides these a large number are dependent upon their labor in various ways. This strong force cannot be easily conquered. They are a well educated people, and they understand their combined interests so well, that they will submit without murmuring, to any necessary reduction of profits or wages, rather than to see the industry, upon which their existence depends, departing from their hands.

Let those economists who prate of the "encouragement of foreign paupers" consider that these stalwart laborers and their families are consumers of our produce. The profit on the shipbuilding inures to them, the profit on the raising of grain to us, and then there is the profit on the transportation. This, we stupidly insist shall be theirs likewise. On the whole business we modestly claim but one-third, voluntarily surrendering the freight to England!

Upon the banks of the Clyde there are about thirty shipbuilding firms, all doing a flourishing business, but the giants among them are:—

John Elder, Glasgow;
Barclay & Curle, "
A. & J. Inglis, "
Robert Napier & Sons, "
J. & G. Thompson, "
Tod & MacGregor, "
John Reid, Port Glasgow;
Duncan & Co., " "
Henderson & Co., Renfrew;
William Denny & Brothers, Dumbarton;
Caird & Co., Greenock.
Scott & Co., "
Steel & Co., "

By either one or the other of these firms, steamships have been and are being continually turned out for the—

Cunard Line,
Inman's Line,
Allan's Line,
Royal Mail West India Line,
Panama Line,
French Transatlantic Line,
Spanish and West India Mail Line,
Hamburg and United States Line,
Bremen and United States Line,
Peninsula and Oriental Company's Line,
British India Company's Line,
Austrian Lloyds Line,
Brazilian, Chinese and Japanese coast lines,

and others too numerous to mention.

This list will show not only that these great companies select this locality as their best and cheapest building place, but it will show that all maritime nations, including the Chinese, avail themselves of the Clyde for their own advantage. *All nations, excepting free and enlightened America!*

France, Spain, Italy, Germany,—even Brazil, China and Japan,—are in advance of us in this branch of political economy!

Add to the above list the hundreds of sailing ships, and numerous steamers, besides those for British and foreign navies here built by contract, and some idea may be formed of the business done upon the Clyde.

I have before me an official "Report upon the vital, social, and economic statistics of Glasgow for 1868, by William West Watson, F. S. S., City Chamberlain."

Mr. Watson justly remarks: "In my Report of last year I ventured to express an opinion that the prospects of 1868, for the shipbuilding interests of the Clyde, seemed very hopeful. The result has greatly exceeded these anticipations, and the year has produced almost the largest amount of new tonnage of any upon record; — it has closed also with sanguine prospects of continued success. In point of fact, the remark may be made with some degree of pride, *that the shipbuilding of the Clyde exceeds that of all the other ports of Great Britain combined.* Only a limited portion of the tonnage constructed on the banks of the Clyde is on account of native owners. The Clyde has acquired a wide-spread fame, and it is worthily maintained upon every sea; otherwise, shipowners of every nation,* as well as our own and other governments, would not, year after year, resort hither to have their work performed.

"There must unquestionably be an advantage obtained on the one side, and a preference afforded on the other, either in regard to economy as to cost or durability as to construction, or in elegance as to form and figure, or probably all combined, which can enable the Clyde thus successfully to hold her own against all competitors."

---

* Mr. Watson is correct,—with the exception of the United States.

He then subjoins the following tables, and adds a commentary upon them, which cannot be more clearly expressed than in his own words:—

"The following table exhibits the particulars, arranged in groups, of all the new vessels which have been launched upon the Clyde from Rutherglen to Greenock, during the year 1868.

NEW VESSELS LAUNCHED ON THE CLYDE DURING THE YEAR 1868.

IRON STEAMERS under 100 tons each, .	12	617		
" from 100 to 500 tons each,	32	8,255		
" from 500 to 1000 "	14	9,914		
" from 1000 to 2000 "	17	26,749		
" from 2000 to 3000 "	4	9,480		
" from 300 and upwards, .	9	27,653		
			88	82,668
IRON SAILING SHIPS under 500 tons each,	11	2,170		
" from 500 to 1000 "	22	16,655		
" from 1000 to 2000 "	34	43,105		
			67	61,930
COMPOSITE STEAMERS under 500 tons each,	2	928		
" " 500 to 1000 "	4	2,882		
			6	3,810
COMPOSITE SAILING SHIPS under 500 tons each, .	3	694		
" " 500 to 1000 " .	12	9,761		
" " 1000 to 2000 " .	3	3,448		
			18	13,903
WOODEN STEAMERS, ...			0	0
WOODEN SAILING VESSELS, ...			2	270
ARMOR-CLAD TURRET WAR-SHIPS,—"De Buffel," and "De Tyer,"			2	3,086
COMPOSITE GUNBOATS, ...			4	1,369
IRON STEAM HOPPER BARGES, ...			8	1,950
IRON STEAM DREDGERS, ...			2	485
IRON STEAM FERRY BOAT, ...			1	100
			197	169,571

"The next table exhibits, also in groups, the particulars of all the vessels which were either actually in process of construction or under contract, at the close of the year 1868.

VESSELS IN PROCESS OF CONSTRUCTION OR CONTRACTED FOR, AT 31st DECEMBER, 1868.

Iron Steamers,—ranging from 40 up to 3,160 tons each,	55	69,876
Iron Sailing Ships,	40	38,689
Composite Steamers,	3	1,805
" Sailing Ships,	14	13,317
Wooden Steamers,	0	0
" Sailing Ships,	4	656
Armor-Clad War-Ships,—"Invincible," "Audacious," and "Hotspur,"	3	10,188
Composite Lightship, for India,	1	287
	120	134,818

"To a non-professional observer, or indeed to almost any one whomsoever, the tables given above will furnish only a very vague and indefinite idea of something which is remarkably extensive; but the matter becomes somewhat, although not much more intelligible, or at least it is apparently more capable of being grasped, if we express it in the form of a pecuniary value. Well, then, some idea of the vast magnitude and importance of the shipbuilding trade of the Clyde may possibly be realized, if we reflect that the value of the vessels enumerated in the first of these tables was upwards of three and a quarter millions of pounds sterling; and that of the latter—

those in course of construction — somewhat above three millions sterling.

"I need scarcely again advert to the continued development of the employment of iron in shipbuilding, as contrasted with that of any other material upon the banks of the Clyde. Indeed, a glance at the two tables last exhibited elicits the fact that while not a single wooden steamer was built or was under contract in 1868, only two sailing vessels built of wood were launched during the year, and only four were contracted for at its close. Upon the other hand, the composite construction — especially for sailing ships — advances in favor, as nearly 14,000 tons of the latter were launched during the year, while upwards of 13,000 tons were in process. Yet all these present but an insignificant proportion to the array of figures which the iron statistics exhibit, and which may be summarized thus:—

Launched in 1868 —

Iron Steamers and Sailing Ships, ...	151,688 tons.
Composite do do, ...	17,613 "
Wooden Sailing Ships, ...	270 "

Under contract, or in process of construction, 31st December, 1868 —

Iron Steamers and Sailing Ships, ...	118,753 tons.
Composite do do, ...	15,409 "
Wooden Sailing Ships, ...	656 " "

The "composite," referred to in Mr. Watson's tables, is a system little known with us. It combines many of the advantages of iron and the only one of wood. A composite vessel is constructed with iron frame and wooden planks, which are fastened to the metal ribs with composition screws. Oak is unserviceable, as it contains a pyroligneous acid which eats the iron and reacts by rendering the wood "ironsick." Teak is generally used, as instead of this acid, it has an oily nature which is a preservative for both substances. Composite vessels have the same room for stowage as those of iron, although they are perhaps not so durable. But they can be sheathed with copper so that they are not liable to the objection of fouling.

I have addressed a note to Messrs. William Denny & Brothers, one of the firms already referred to, making the following inquiries:—

I. What is the average price for skilled labor in shipbuilding?

II. What is the price of ordinary labor?

III. What is the cost of iron per ton?—pig, sheet and wrought.

IV. What is the price of coal?

V. What is the cost of labor on a steamer of 3,000 tons?

VI. What is the cost of material on the same?

VII. What is the cost of engines of 400 nominal horse power?

VIII. What is the cost, per ton, of an iron sailing ship ready for sea?

IX. What is the rule for calculating British tonnage?

X. What is the difference in capacity between wooden and iron vessels of the same exterior dimensions?

XI. What is the cost of composite vessels, as compared with those of iron?

XII. What is the comparative cost of wire and hemp rigging?

To which they have obligingly returned the following replies:—

"I. Twenty-five to twenty-eight shillings per week.

II. Fifteen to eighteen shillings per week.

III. Pig iron, £2 17*s.*; plates, £8 5*s.*; bar (common,) £7; bar (best,) £8. Of course, they vary.

IV. Ten to twelve shillings per ton.

V. About £21,500.

VI. About £40,000.

VII. £22,000. Everything depends on the style and finish of ship and engines; but the answers to 5, 6, 7, refer to a first-class ship, — the engines complete, and well found in spare gear. A four hundred horse-power nominal engine should indicate 2,600 effective, and would drive a good form of ship thirteen knots on trial. A rough way of arriving at the cost of a first-class screw passenger steamer, is to calculate the gross tonnage at £28 to £30. This would include engines capable of giving a speed of eleven to twelve knots.

VIII. £14 10*s.* to £15, according to finish.

IX. The customs rule is *generally* explained by calculating the internal capacity of the vessel into cubic feet, and dividing by 100, the result being considered tons.

X. An iron ship of say 1,000 tons register, would carry 200 tons more of measurement than a wooden ship of the same dimensions. Such is the experience of Mr. Henderson, of Glasgow, who is largely engaged in the Australian trade.

XI. Composite vessels from £2 to £3 more per ton than iron.

XII. There is a saving in weight by using wire rope of one-third. Thus, 3½-inch wire rope, of weight per fathom 10 lbs., is equal to 8-inch hemp rope of weight per fathom 15 lbs. The present price of wire is thirty-seven shillings per cwt. The price of hemp rope per cwt. is forty-two shillings. Upon the difference there is a saving in money of 33 per cent."

My esteemed friend, Mr. Edwards, of the Boston Atlantic Works, whose company has been largely engaged in building ships and machinery for the Government, informs me that the American price of

Pig iron is	$41.00	currency per ton.
Plates, ...	101.00	" "
Bar, (common,)	92.50	" "
Bar, (best,)	97.50	" "
And that skilled labor with them is	$3	per day.
Ordinary labor, ...	2	"

On both sides the water the day's labor is considered as of 10 hours.

Mr. Edwards says that he is persuaded that if the Government will remit the duties on iron, he can build ships as cheap as they do in Scotland. He does not say that there are coal and iron mines in East Boston, within a stone's throw of his furnaces, nor does he say that his men will submit to a reduction of one-half their wages.

I have not deemed it necessary to propound any questions as to the cost of wooden ships. Hereabout such vessels are obsolete, and I doubt if most of the builders in England and Scotland could give us any information on that point, to which they are as indifferent as they would be in regard to the items that entered into the construction of Noah's Ark. Not only are all ships built principally of iron, but the tendency is to discard wood altogether in their construction. The last answer, relating to wire rigging, shows how hemp is entirely dispensed with, except for running gear. Wood is no longer needed for lowermasts, bowsprit and yards, all of which spars are infinitely stronger, lighter, cheaper, and more durable than wood.

Decks are sometimes made of iron plates instead of planks, as in the case of the London and New York line of steamers, and it should not be long before one greater benefit than any thus far enumerated shall accrue to humanity in the absolute freedom from the slightest danger of fire at sea. Every table, chair, bulkhead and berth fixture, in the cabin, forecastle and steerage, may be made of thin or corrugated iron, and the mattrasses may be saturated with fire-proof preparations. As emigrant ships may thus be made secure from one of the greatest perils to which such vessels are exposed, the law should compel them to adopt these precautions.

I have spoken of the Clyde as the shipbuilding emporium of the world. Let us see how the English regard it, as incidentally appears from a recent article in the *Pall Mall Gazette*.

"THE SHIPBUILDING TRADE. — The cause of the decline of shipbuilding on the Thames seems to be fully accounted for on studying a table prepared by Mr. John Glover, showing the daily rate of wages on the Thames, Wear and Clyde, of carpenters, joiners, platers, caulkers, riveters, painters, riggers, sailmakers, boilermakers, engineers, turners, and pattern workers. The cost of one day's labor from those combined crafts is, on the Thames, 72*s.*; on the Clyde, 58*s.* 8*d.* The Thames price is 22.72 per cent. higher than the Clyde. Moreover, it appears that Thames workmanship is no better than that on the Clyde and Mersey, or Tyne and Wear; and that Government and other contracts are naturally no longer restricted to the Thames. The difference in the rate of wages is aggravated by the extent to which work is done by the "piece" in the northern yards. Iron work on the Clyde is nearly all so done, and nine-tenths of it on the Wear. The comparative disuse of wood in the construction of ships has also materially affected this industry. Formerly all vessels were built of wood. Coal and iron, and the cost thereof, were not then very important items in their construction. Now a steamer built of wood is a rarity, and nearly all large sailing vessels are built either entirely of iron, or of iron in the interior, with a wooden skin. The disuse of wood, and the greatly increased use of iron, favors the rivers in close proximity to the banks of which iron is manufactured, and where coal, so important an item in all work with iron, is also found proximate and therefore cheap. The reason why Thames wages did not fall with the decline of trade, until such a level had been reached as would have enabled Thames masters to compete successfully with other rivers, is attributed by Mr. Glover to the decrees of the "union." They fixed a limit below which wages ought not, in their opinion, to fall. They succeeded thus far. Wages remain nominally high. But there is no work; trade is destroyed. It is perhaps, he adds, an extreme illustration of what happens when the men become masters."

What then? It is true that London and Glasgow are under the same government, and so the cases are not exactly parallel; but they are enough so to suggest the question, should the London merchants, now that ships can no longer be built in their district, insist that the Glasgow people, who do build them, should continue to own them, and take to themselves all the profit of their freight as well as of their construction?

Would such a resolution promote the building of a single ship or steamer on the Thames? Would it not inevitably force the control of all their foreign trade into the hands of their provincial neighbors, and the ownership of their continental steamship lines upon foreigners? And yet this is American policy,—it is our system of "protecting" Englishmen, Dutchmen, Germans and Frenchmen against ourselves!

I have now done with arguments and statistics. It may be said that if our navigation laws were repealed the builders on the Clyde will benefit thereby, and that this fact will weigh against the measure. But I cannot believe that my countrymen are such dogs in the manger, or that they will refuse to ride in the "car of Time," which carries "bright improvement" with it, merely because there may be other passengers on the train.

Doubtless a still greater impulse would be given to shipbuilding here, if they are disposed to come over and participate in its benefit. I know these hospitable Scotsmen well enough to be assured that they would give those Americans of their own craft, who cannot make a living at home, a hearty welcome "to the land of cakes." They are not slow to admit that they can learn some things from our builders of the beam engine, and from our artistic modellers and decorators.

In conclusion, it is from all considerations of national economy, and those totally irrespective of tariff or free trade as the revenue will be affected thereby otherwise than for the general good, that I urge you and your committee, in your forthcoming report, to advocate *the total repeal of the old law, and to couple with it the permission for our ships to take their stores out of bond free of duty.*

In this way, and in this way only, we may hope for the revival of our commerce, and for a participation with England in the sovereignty of the seas.

I am, Sir, very respectfully,

Your obedient servant,

JOHN CODMAN.

Hon. John Lynch, *Chairman.*

While this letter was in press, an auction sale has been made of the Boston steamers "Ontario" and "Erie," referred to on page 10.

When these wooden ships were in process of construction, the files of the *Boston Post* will bear witness to the prediction that they would ultimately cost double the amount for which two steamers of equal capacity could be built of iron in Scotland.

It now appears that their liabilities for building, and for the various liens upon them, fall little short of $2,000,000! There was but one bid for them, and they were sold for $256,217 each. Only one man could be found who wanted cheap elephants.

Now, it may be claimed, with absolute certainty, that ships which will carry as much as these, that will steam as fast on one-half the coal they consume, and will be serviceable vessels when these are rotten, can be built on the Clyde for £75,000 each. Instead of furnishing so costly an argument, had the stockholders exerted their influence to get the prohibitory navigation law repealed, Boston might now have had a successful line of her own, instead of "protecting" the British flag, under which she is now obliged to ship and receive her merchandise.

www.ingramcontent.com/pod-product-compliance
Lightning Source LLC
LaVergne TN
LVHW011124110826
845150LV00008B/2240

* 9 7 8 1 4 1 8 1 9 5 3 5 9 *